Harping On

Harping On

POEMS 1985-1995

———

Carolyn Kizer

COPPER CANYON PRESS

Publication of this book is supported by a grant from the National Endowment for the Arts and a grant from the Lannan Foundation. Additional support to Copper Canyon Press has been provided by the Andrew W. Mellon Foundation, the Lila Wallace–Reader's Digest Fund, and the Washington State Arts Commission. Copper Canyon Press is in residence with Centrum at Fort Worden State Park.

Library of Congress Cataloging-in-Publication Data
Kizer, Carolyn
Harping on: poems 1985–1996 / by Carolyn Kizer
p. cm.
ISBN 1-55659-114-4 (cloth) 1-55659-115-2 (pbk.)
I. Title.
PS3521.I9H37 1996
811'.54 – dc20   96-25300

COPPER CANYON PRESS
P.O. BOX 271, PORT TOWNSEND, WASHINGTON 98368

Acknowledgments

"Marriage Song" and "Reunion" appeared in *Antæus*. "Twelve O'Clock," "Halation," "Gerda," and "Anniversaries" appeared in *The Paris Review*. "The Valley of the Fallen," "Ingathering," "Pearl," "Medicine," "Arthur's Party," and "Poem for Your Birthday," appeared in *Poetry*. "Lost in Translation" appeared in *The Southern Review*. "An American Beauty" appeared in *The Yale Review*. "On a Line from Valéry" appeared in *The Princeton Library Journal*. "Parents' Pantoum" appeared on the editorial page of *The New York Times*. "In Hell with Virg and Dan" appeared in *13th Moon*. The translation of "Tirade for the Next-to-Last Act" appeared in *The American Poetry Review*, and subsequently in the book of Nina Cassian's poems, *Life Sentences*. "Fearful Women" appeared in *Hubbub*, "Election Day, 1984" in the *Southern California Anthology*, and "Cultural Evolution" in *The Epigramatist*. "Index, a Mountain" appeared in *Verse*. "What is True" and "Maryam" appeared in *Shenandoah*.

"Twelve O'Clock" also appeared in *Pushcart*, and in *The Best American Poetry, 1992* (ed. Charles Simic). "Marriage Song" appeared in *The Best Poetry, 1991* (ed. Mark Strand). "On a Line from Valéry" appeared in *The Best American Poetry, 1995* (ed. Richard Howard).

"Suppressing the Evidence" was written for the anthology, *Season of Dead Water*, about the Exxon oil-spill disaster. "On a Line from Valéry" was written about the Gulf War.

for EMMA

Contents

Harping On

The Valley of the Fallen

*In this Valley of the Fallen, one finds the soul of Spain,
beautiful and severe. When the great bronze doors –
eleven tons each – swing open for state ceremonies, ten
thousand worshippers can assemble there at a time...
Only Franco and his intimates know the cost of this
monument with its adjacent Benedictine monastery
and its lavishly fitted center for social studies...*
— BENJAMIN WELLES

1

My new friend, Maisie, who works where I work,
A big, pleasant woman, all elbows and peasant skirts,
Has a young child, and debts, and struggles on her own.
Not twenty-one, I am her confidante.
Gallant, intrepid, she soldiers on;
But in the ladies' restroom, or when we munch
Our sandwiches at our adjoining desks,
Her bitterness erupts: the bum! the bum
Who, when she was pregnant, knocked her down,
Stole money from her purse to spend on drink,
And still harasses her with drunken calls
In 1946.
One day I have to ask,

"Maisie, why did you ever marry him?"
Gazing into her large, pale-blue eyes
That brim with rue: "Well, you see,
He fought in the Abraham Lincoln Brigade."
"Oh," I say. I would have done it too.

When I say I wouldn't go to Spain
Till Franco died, I've told a whole
Biography: my age, my politics,
My Red – and red-haired – mother whose green eyes
Sparked at the sins of tyrants anywhere;
My father, who was counsel for the poor
And radical, against the bigot and the hater,
Burnt up the courtroom with his tongue of flame
(McCarthy got around to us much later).
So Spain burst in while I was still a child:
My introduction to the world.

At seventeen, my first love, Frank,
Gave me some records, battered seventy-eights,
The off-key songs of the International Brigade.
I still sing them, remember all the words
In Spanish, French and German:
The Peat Bog Soldiers, accompanied by harmonica
In a Barcelona basement; *"Freiheit!"* we sing
To a guitar. You can still hear
The thuds of the bombardment.
I sing and listen till the tears run down.
That's forty years of tears.

> *Seven hundred men worked every day for ten years*
> *to dig this place, and many of them were political*
> *prisoners of the regime. Franco lies now in a tomb*
> *before the high altar, and all day long the monks, the*
> *nuns and the soldiers file through...*
> – JAN MORRIS, 1979

3

My husband and I shudder a bit and smile –
He's an architect, has seen photographs
Of Franco's grandiose memorial,
The Valley of the Fallen.
At first the thought appalled, but we've decided
It's part of architecture, part of history too,
So we drive the road from the Escorial,
Climb tiers and tiers of stairs,
Take in the view.

The whole vast place is virtually empty
Save for a handful of tourists like ourselves.
Down the long gloomy hall, not as grotesque
As we expected; muted lights;
Chisels score the vault so that we'll know
They tunneled through the mountain,
Franco's slave labor, some the very men
Who fought him.
                   But at least they buried him!

We reach the circular altar with its flame;
First, the grave of José Antonio,
Primo de Rivera, who fathered the Falange,
On it a huge ugly wreath
From the Italian Fascisti.
I wouldn't be suprised if asps crawled out
Beneath its leaves of artificial bronze,
But still – at my age – am surprised
That the old evil lives.

Behind this, the Caudillo's stone.
I say, "I'm going to spit upon his grave."
John tilts his head towards the honor guard,
Impassive, armed, white-gloved.
He knows me well enough
To know I just might do it. But instead,
I speak a curse: *Franco, I spit upon your grave.*

On the way out, we use the men's room
And the ladies' room, try to buy postcards
But it's closing time;
Then drive back to Madrid,
Where I read poems to the kids
At the University,
In a classroom scarred with revolutionary slogans
Four years old, that no one's bothered to erase.
I sing of Lorca, Chile, and Neruda
And the wars we lose.

> *The Valle de los Caidos can be included in your trip to*
> *the Escorial... Like a modern-day Valhalla, the crypt is*
> *cut through 853 feet of living rock and surmounted by*
> *a 492 foot cross of reinforced concrete faced with stone*
> *(with an elevator to the top). Admission 75 pesetas*
> *with two in a car; 100 pesetas for more than two.*
> *Open 9–7:30.*
>   – FODOR'S *Spain,* 1984

6

Ingathering

The poets are going home now,
After the years of exile,
After the northern climates
Where they worked, lectured, remembered,
Where they shivered at night
In an indifferent world.
Where God was the god of business,
And men would violate the poets' moon,
And even the heavens become zones of war.

The poets are going home
To the blood-haunted villages,
To the crumbling walls, still pocked
With a spray of bullets;
To the ravine, marked with a new cross,
Where their brother died.
No one knows the precise spot where they shot him,
But there is a place now to gather, to lay wreaths.
The poets will bring flowers.

The poets are coming home
To the cafés, to the life of the streets at twilight,
To slip among the crowds and greet their friends;
These young poets, old now, limping, who lean on a cane:
Or the arm of a grandchild, peer with opaque eyes
At the frightening city, the steel and concrete towers
Sprung up in their absence.
Yet from open doorways comes the odor of grapes
Fermented, of fish, of oil, of pimiento…

The poets have come home
To the melodious language
That settles in their heads like moths alighting,
This language for which they starved
In a world of gutterals,
Crude monosyllables barked by strangers.

Now their own language enfolds them
With its warm vocables.
The poets are home.

Yes, they have come back
To look up at the yellow moon,
Cousin of that cold orb that only reflected
Their isolation.
They have returned to the olives, the light,
The sage-scented meadows,
The white-washed steps, the tubs of geraniums,
The sere plains, the riverbanks spread with laundry,
The poppies, the vineyards, the bones of mountains.

Yes, poets, welcome home
To your small country
Riven by its little war
(as the world measures these events),
A country that remembers heroes and tears;
Where, in your absence, souls kept themselves alive
By whispering your words.
Now you smile at everything, even the priests, the militia,
The patient earth that is waiting to receive you.

Election Day, 1984

Did you ever see someone cold-cock a blind nun?
Well, I did. Two helpful idiots
Steered her across the tarmac to her plane
And led her smack into the wing.
She deplaned with two black eyes & a crooked wimple,
Bruised proof that the distinction is not simple
Between ineptitude and evil.
Today, with the President's red button playing
Such a prominent role,
Though I can't vote for it, I wonder
If evil could be safer, on the whole.

Gerda

Gud, som haver barnen kär,
Se till mig som liten är.
Vart jag mig i världen vänder
Står min lycka i Guds händer.

    — OLD SWEDISH CHILDREN'S PRAYER

Down the long curving walk you trudge to the street,
Stoop-shouldered in defeat, a cardboard suitcase
In each hand. *Gerda, don't leave!* the child cries
From the porch, waving and weeping; her stony mother
Speaks again of the raise in salary
Denied. Gerda demands ten dollars more
Than the twenty-five a month she has been paid
To sew, cook, keep house, dress and undress the child,
Bathe the child with the rough scaly hands
she cleans in Clorox; sing to the child
In Swedish, teach her to pray, to count on her toes
In Swedish. Forty years on, the child still knows how,
Is a great hit with children under seven, in Sweden,
Singing a folk song, praying, counting toes.
For twenty-five dollars a month in 1933
Gerda makes for the child her favorite, *fattigmand,*
A mix of flour, milk and eggs you cut in strips,
Then fry in fat, then dust with sugar
(the child helps Gerda cook so she knows that).
In Stockholm the child will inquire of *fattigmand,*
But like lost Gerda it does not exist.

Deep in the Depression, the child fears for her
As Gerda trudges down the walk, four blocks to the bus,
Then the train to Minneapolis. *What will she do?*
Gerda, trained as a nurse, found no work before
She came to us. Twenty-five dollars a month
To sew a quilt for the child, covered with fabulous
Animals feather-stitched in blue and white;
Now after fifty years it hangs on the wall

Of the child's grandchild, in a Chicago house.
Then, when the child awoke, addled and drunk with nightmare,
She dragged the quilt from her cot,
Stumbled sniffling into Gerda's room,
To be taken into her bed, soothed back to sleep
By the rough, antiseptic hands.

The child wakes up to naked light.
Ageless Gerda's steel-grey bob shakes into place
(she owns no mirror);
Blind Gerda gropes for her steel-rimmed spectacles
As the child sees, with fascinated love,
The curd in the corner of each of Gerda's eyes.
It is a magic substance the child has improvised
On a favorite tale: Hans Christian Andersen's
Snow Queen. She thinks of it as the good cream curd,
The reverse of the splinter in the eye
of little Kay: everyone, like the brave child in the story,
Everyone like Gerda.

Modest Gerda dresses in the closet,
Then the two on tiptoe steal to the child's room
So the stout handsome mother will not waken.
Then Gerda bathes the child, scrubs her hard all over
With the loofah, dries her carefully on the big warm towel,
Pulls on her panties of white cotton, then the dress,
Smelling deliciously of Gerda's iron, the dress
Gerda smocked at night while the household slept,
Then the pastel sweater Gerda knitted her.
The child sits on the edge of the bed while Gerda
Brushes then twists the child's fair hair
Into two fat braids secured with rubber bands.

The child, so much fairer than her parents, nearly believes
She's Swedish; is pleased then, and forty years on
To be taken for Scandinavian: Gerda's own.
Now Gerda pulls up the white anklets, fastens the sandals.
Down to the pantry! – where the child climbs into her chair.

Gerda sets three places, one for the child,
One for the child's imaginary playmate, one for her.
And they eat the lovely oatmeal Gerda cooked the night before.

Thirty years on, her father will remark,
Your mother was jealous
So we let her go. Of course I could have raised her wages,
Gerda ran the house! The child's throat fills with bile
As, casually, he continues: *I always let your mother*
Decide these matters. Smug, he often used that phrase
As if the abdication of his parenthood
Had been a sacrifice. What did he know
Of the child's needs or passions?
So Gerda left the house, the yard, the garden,
The child's home long torn down,
A place that no longer exists.
Thirty-five years on, the child stumbles among the weeds
In search of the path down which her Gerda walked
Or a trace of the porch where she once stood, bereft.

The child's eighth year, like Gerda, disappeared.
Hazy recall of illness:
Asthma, the wheeze, the struggle for breath,
And the louder rhythmic wheeze of oxygen...
Of the weeks in bed, lying inert, nothing remains,
Only the pallid joys of recovery,
Jello and milk, ice cream three times a day
(was this a bribe?);
Dreamily sucking a spoonful of melting vanilla:
Only these splinters of a vanished year.

It must have been then that the ice-house dream began,
Her first and last recurring dream:
The child stands in a little room of ice;
Outside a song begins, impossibly nostalgic,
Played on a concertina or harmonium.
As the dream goes on
Slowly, slowly the walls move in, the ceiling presses down

Till she is encased in a kind of upright coffin
Of milky iridescent ice. Entranced by a vision
Of green hills and pure blue skies without,
She conceives freedom and flight!
She must memorize the tune as the ice moves in
To touch her on every side and on her head.
As the last, haunting note is played
The child wakes up. Of course the tune is gone.
It is always gone.

For ten years the child nurtures a secret plan:
A last she boards a train for the East,
Waits for the layover in Minneapolis,
Hurries to a pay phone, armed with change,
Opens the directory,
Faints to see four columns, closely printed,
Of Gerda Johnsons. *How could there be more than one?*
Ranging her nickels on the metal counter.
She calls from the top
As the hands of the clock spin round.
Gerda! Gerda! Half-a-page
With answers none, or ancient whispery Norse voices
Down a tunnel of years, and oceans crossed
And cold home villages abandoned long ago.
Then she runs out of change and time. A train to catch.
She weeps at terminated hope, nourished for so long,
As the old filmstrip runs again:

Gerda, you trudge down the walk forever;
The child, no matter how she calls and cries,
Cannot catch up.
Now from another life she summons you
Out of the earth or aether, wherever you are,
Gerda, come back, to nurse your desolate child.

Pearl

Every Thursday Pearl arrived in her old Model A
with a satchel of lotions cremes and balms
    to make over Mother.
Fresh from her bath, Mother lay on her ample belly
as Pearl pummeled, rubbed, massaged
    the firm fleshy back of Mother
till it turned from sweaty peach to glistening crimson.

Then they move from her bed to the still-steamy bathroom,
    where
Mother bends over the basin as Pearl soaps her head;
    and the witness-child
stares at the face of her mother, upside-down
    between brown curtains of hair.
Pearl, busy as any nurse or minister,
    moves briskly from sink to chair,
applies the harsh-colored henna the child abhors.

Pearl seems to ignore the child's disapproving frown;
    the child can't catch her eye,
though Mother's, luminous and green, are transfixed with pity
as she attends to Pearl's inconsequent chatter;
    beneath it, Mother and child
hear the drone of the terrible dirge that is never over,
the song of a fatally wounded Columbine
    with her crazed painted smile:

Pearl, frantic with a croupy daughter,
    frightened of losing days
of work with Madame Patenaud, her termagant employer,
had forced her own little girl to swallow her medicine.
But what was hastily thrust between the child's burning lips
was Lysol. The little girl abandoned her.
    Pearl is alone forever.

Now this child imagines Pearl as hollow,
    a decorated funerary urn
set on an altar not to God but to Beauty.
Pearl paints Mother's toenails propped on the sink.
    Why hadn't she died?
But perhaps she had – and it's a ghost of her
who pearls these fingers, toes; then later paces
the nightmares of the child. Desolation and desertion!
Pearl's ivory face averted as the child begs mercy
    from the bleak desert of dream.

But now, swathed like a houri in a heavy towel,
    Mother leans back in her chair
while Pearl stirs magic in a jar: brown sticky unguent.
Pearl's mentor, Madame Patenaud, in long-ago Los Angeles
was a genius with cremes and lotions; even today
    Pearl's voice hushes with awe
as she applies the secret formula reeking of tar
(the child's nose never forgets), a potion which,
faithfully used, confers eternal youth.

She would be Ponce de Leon to Pearl's elixir,
eternally youthful Mama, fat and beautiful,
    transfixed
as Time is cheated; Pearl swabs her face, dabs it with ice.
They study her reflection, Pearl nods
with satisfaction; only a tiny frown
as Pearl tweezes a single hair from Mother's arching brows:
    a Japanese master gardener
who plucks one needle from a famous pine.

The child senses the bond between these two,
the tragic and the laughing Muse – she, bare-faced now,
an empty canvas on which Pearl plies her skills
except that it is a speaking canvas, critical
of its creator, who reinvents her look
    as the child is shut out.

She who grimaces hideously in the mirror,
puffing her cheeks or putting out her tongue,
is stuck, she fears forever, with this pudding oval
    which no hand molds.
Oh, she will cartoon herself with bloody lipstick
    stolen from Mama,
but scorns her own lack of skill – presses Mother and Pearl
    to be let in.

As we grow older, Mother, you close the distances
between us, with kisses, dresses, tiny conspiracies.
We cuddle beneath one comforter, serene and mild.
But Pearl, O Pearl, I would have been your heart's fulfillment.
I was your prodigy, your dream of life.
    I was your murdered child.

Reunion

For more than thirty years we hadn't met.
I remembered the bright query of your face,
That single-minded look, intense and stern,
Yet most important – how could I forget? –
Was what you taught me inadvertently
(tutored by books and parents, even more
By my own awe at what was yet to learn):
The finest intellect can be a bore.

At this, perhaps our final interview,
Still luminous with your passion to instruct,
You speak to that recalcitrant pupil who
Inhaled the chalk-dust of your rhetoric.
I nod, I sip my wine, I praise your view,
Grateful, my dear, that I escaped from you.

An American Beauty

As you described your mastectomy in calm detail
and bared your chest so I might see
the puckered scar,
"They took a hatchet to your breast!" I said. "What an
Amazon you are."

When we were girls we climbed Mt. Tamalpais
chewing bay leaves we had plucked
along the way;
we got high all right, from animal pleasure in each other,
shouting to the sky.

On your houseboat we tried to ignore the impossible guy
you had married to enrage your family,
a typical ploy.
We were great fools let loose in the No Name bar
on Sausalito's bay.

In San Francisco we'd perch on a waterfront pier
chewing sourdough and cheese, swilling champagne,
kicking our heels;
crooning lewd songs, hooting like seagulls,
we bayed with the seals.

Then you married someone in Mexico,
broke up in two weeks, didn't bother to divorce,
claimed it didn't count.
You dumped number three, fled to Albany
to become a pedant.

Averse to domesticity, you read for your Ph.D.
Your four-year-old looked like a miniature
John Lennon.
You fed him peanut butter from the jar and raised him
on Beowulf and Grendel.

Much later in New York we reunited;
in an elevator at Sak's a woman asked for
your autograph.
You glowed like a star, like Anouk Aimée
at forty, close enough.

Your pedantry found its place in the Women's Movement.
You rose fast, seen suddenly as the morning star;
wrote the ERA
found the right man at last, a sensitive artist;
flying too high

not to crash. When the cancer caught you
you went on talk shows to say you had no fear
or faith.
In Baltimore we joked on your bed as you turned into
a witty wraith.

When you died I cleaned out your bureau drawers:
your usual disorder; an assortment of gorgeous wigs
and prosthetic breasts
tossed in garbage bags, to spare your gentle spouse.
Then the bequests

you had made to every friend you had!
For each of us a necklace or a ring.
A snapshot for me:
We two, barefoot in chiffon, laughing amid blossoms
your last wedding day.

FOR ANN LONDON

On a Line from Valéry

Tout le ciel vert se meurt
Le dernier arbre brûle.

The whole green sky is dying. The last tree flares
With a great burst of supernatural rose
Under a canopy of poisonous airs.

Could we imagine our return to prayers
To end in time before time's final throes,
The green sky dying as the last tree flares?

But we were young in judgement, old in years
Who could make peace: but it was war we chose,
To spread its canopy of poisoning airs.

Not all our children's pleas and women's fears
Could steer us from this hell. And now God knows
His whole green sky is dying as it flares.

Our crops of wheat have turned to fields of tares.
This dreadful century staggers to its close
And the sky dies for us, its poisoned heirs.

All rain was dust. Its granules were our tears.
Throats burst as universal winter rose
To kill the whole green sky, the last tree bare
Beneath its canopy of poisoned air.

THE GULF WAR

20

Suppressing the Evidence

Alaska oil spill, I edit you out.
You are too terrible to think about.
I X, I double-X you out.
The repeated floods in Bangladesh:
The starving poor that stare at us,
Stare with plaintive smiles,
Smiles without hope
As they clutch a bulbous-bellied child,
I erase your dark faces.
I edit you out.

From the dark windows of their limousines
The rich long since have waved their ringed hands,
Said Abracadabra, to disappear the poor.
Their streets are swept clear
So the homeless are sucked down the dirty drains.
Only their reflections in the tinted glass
Stare back in their complacent discontent:
The blind rich, in their blind car.

On Madison a young emaciated man
In a threadbare jacket, shivers in the snow.
Help me. Please. I have no place to go.
I hold out a dollar bill between his face and mine
Like the fan of an old Japanese courtesan,
Then hurry past as his face turns to smoke.

I flee the city, back to my comfortable farm
In the valley of wine. I drink the wine.
I do not turn on the news.
I and the wine will blot it out.
And we erase more and more of the world's terrible map
How may we bear witness, as we should?

I must hold in my mind one small dead otter pup.

Fearful Women

Arms and the girl I sing – O rare
arms that are braceleted and white and bare

arms that were lovely Helen's, in whose name
Greek slaughtered Trojan. Helen was to blame.

Scape-nanny call her; wars for turf
and profit don't sound glamorous enough.

Mythologize your women! None escape.
Europe was named from an act of bestial rape:

Eponymous girl on bull-back, he intent
on scattering sperm across a continent.

Old Zeus refused to take the rap.
It's not his name in big print on the map.

But let's go back to the beginning
when sinners didn't know that they were sinning.

He, one rib short: she lived to rue it
when Adam said to God, "She made me do it."

Eve learned that learning was a dangerous thing
for her: no end of trouble it would bring.

An educated woman is a danger.
Lock up your mate! Keep a submissive stranger

like Darby's Joan, content with church and Kinder,
not like that sainted Joan, burnt to a cinder.

Whether we wield a sceptre or a mop
It's clear you fear that we may get on top.

And if we do – I say it without animus –
It's not from you we learned to be magnanimous.

Halation

A phenomenon...which caused an ambiguous
shimmering brightness to appear on the print
where sunlight and foliage came into contiguity.
   – JANET MALCOLM

My dear, you moved so rapidly through my life
I see you as a ghostly blur;
You are the subject, I the ornament
Eternally crossing cobbles on some *rue*,
Where a covey of pearl umbrellas glistens
And ladies pause – courtesy of Caillebotte – though
This is of an era before we were born.
But the impression is emotionally true:
A sheen of rain, a gray noncommital sky;
Limp banners cling to window frames (Monet);
And the bonnet, shovel-shaped with a crimson brim,
Casts a becoming glow over my face,
No longer young, ambiguous, shimmering.
A bunch of violets tucked at the waist, the figure
Navigates curb and puddle, assisted by
A gentleman in black, a courtly crook of arm:
Poseur and posed, the painter and the painted
Doubly exposed. Now I am reminded

Of a woodland picnic slightly earlier,
You almost fully dressed, I not quite naked;
You in the serge of your reserve
And I as bare as in those disturbing dreams
That reveal our vast uncertainties, including
Those of Giorgione and Manet.
Background figures (us, in fair disguises)
Haunt the middle distance, bosky, green,
Stand witness, even when reclining...
But I am no *Chèrie* but *Liebchen. Liebchen.*
Our expeditions did not end in halycon places.
Instead, all roads led to a sanitary fill

In full sunlight. Nothing ambiguous about that.
We raise champagne in paper cups, toast one another,
Perched on the tailgate of an ugly car.
But the shutter snaps, and we slip into art,
Its negative image: sister into brother.

Once a little coarse, a trifle epicene
(a little too Rouault, whom you admired),
You've silvered over through the passing years.
Now, like a platinum plate, imagination,
That elusive lustre, may transform
A row of poplars to the filaments of desire;
An alley, lit by one gas lamp, the path
To Charon's boat, that ultimate black stream.
This fluid which develops and embalms
Beyond the possibility of alteration,
Is cropped by us, to suit perversities
Of taste and time. Your sinewy arm (Cezanne's)
Seemed to wrap twice around my waist.
Dreamer and dream, in close up confrontation,
The pair emerged as Bonnard's moving blurs.

Touch now, O author of my authorhood,
Your peer at last in contiguity
Before we went our ways and broke the frame.
What happened to us friend? You saw the light,
Not that of haloed streetlamps. Halogen
Impersonally scanned us, banishing
All subtle shadows, a trace of leaves at night.
The hallowed moon, astigmatized before,
Is glowing with a brighter face than ours,
Scored by the years, focused last, and free.

Mud Soup

1. Had the ham bone, had the lentils,
   Got to meat store for the salt pork,
   Got to grocery for the celery.
   Had the onions, had the garlic,
   Borrowed carrots from the neighbor.
   Had the spices, had the parsley.
   One big kettle I had not got;
   Borrowed pot and lid from landlord.

2. Dice the pork and chop the celery,
   Chop the onions, chop the carrots,
   Chop the tender index finger.
   Put the kettle on the burner,
   Drop the lentils into kettle:
   Two quarts water, two cups lentils.
   Afternoon is wearing on.

3. Sauté pork and add the veggies,
   Add the garlic, cook ten minutes,
   Add to lentils, add to ham bone;
   Add the bayleaf, cloves in cheesecloth.
   Add the cayenne! Got no cayenne!
   Got paprika, salt and pepper.
   Bring to boil, reduce heat, simmer.
   Did I say that this is summer?
   Simmer, summer, summer, simmer.
   Mop the floor and suck the finger.
   Mop the brow with old potholder.

4. Time is up! Discard the cheesecloth.
   Force the mixture thru the foodmill
   (having first discarded ham bone).
   Add the lean meat from the ham bone;
   Reheat soup and chop the parsley.
   Now that sweating night has fallen,
   Try at last the finished product:

5. Tastes like mud, the finished product.
   Looks like mud, the finished product.
   Consistency of mud the dinner.
   (Was it lentils, Claiborne, me?)
   Flush the dinner down disposall,
   Say to hell with ham bone, lentils,
   New York Times's recipe.
   Purchase Campbell's. Just add water.
   Concentrate on poetry:
   By the shores of Gitche Gumee
   You can bet the banks were muddy,
   Not like Isle of Innisfree.

Twelve O'Clock

At seventeen I've come to read a poem
At Princeton. Now my young hosts inquire
If I would like to meet Professor Einstein.
But I'm too conscious I have nothing to say
To interest him, the genius fled from Germany just in time.
"Just tell me where I can look at him," I reply.

Mother had scientific training. I did not;
She loved that line of Meredith's about
The army of unalterable law.
God was made manifest to her in what she saw
As the supreme order of the skies.
We lay in the meadow side by side, long summer nights

As she named the stars with awe.
But I saw nothing that was rank on rank,
Heard nothing of the music of the spheres,
But in the bliss of meadow silences
Lying on insects we had mashed without intent,
Found overhead a beautiful and terrifying mess,

Especially in August, when the meteors whizzed and zoomed,
Echoed, in little, by the fireflies in the grass.
Although, small hypocrite, I was seeming to assent,
I was dead certain that uncertainty
Governed the universe, and everything else,
Including Mother's temperament.

A few years earlier, when I was four,
Mother and Father hushed before the Atwater-Kent
As a small voice making ugly noises through the static
Spoke from the grille, church-window-shaped, to them:
"Listen, darling, and remember always;
It's Doctor Einstein broadcasting from Switzerland."

I said, "So what?" This was repeated as a witticism
By my doting parents. I was dumb and mortified.
So when I'm asked if I would like to speak to Einstein
I say I only want to look at him.
"Each day in the library, right at twelve,
Einstein comes out for lunch." So I am posted.

At the precise stroke of noon the sun sends one clear ray
Into the center aisle: He just appears,
Baggy-kneed, sockless, slippered, with
The famous raveling grey sweater;
Clutching a jumble of papers in one hand
And in the other his brown sack of sandwiches.

The ray haloes his head! Blake's vision of God,
Unmuscular, serene, except for the electric hair.
In that flicker of a second our smiles meet:
Vast genius and vast ignorance conjoined;
He fixed, I fluid, in a complicit yet
Impersonal interest. He dematerialized and I left, content.

It was December sixth, exactly when,
Just hours before the Japanese attack
The Office of Scientific R&D
Began "its hugely expanded program of research
Into nuclear weaponry" – racing the Germans who, they feared,
Were far ahead. In fact, they weren't.

Next night, the coach to school; the train, *Express*,
Instead pulls into every hamlet: grim young men
Swarm the platforms, going to enlist.
I see their faces in the sallow light
As the train jolts, then starts up again,
Reaching Penn Station hours after midnight.

At dinner in New York in '44, I hear the name
Of Heisenberg: Someone remarked, "I wonder where he is,
The most dangerous man alive. I hope we get to him in time."

Heisenberg. I kept the name. Were the Germans, still,
Or the Russians, yet, a threat? Uncertainty....
But I felt a thrill of apprehension: Genius struck again.

It is the stroke of twelve – and I suppose
The ray that haloes Einstein haloes me:
White-blonde hair to my waist, almost six feet tall,
In my best and only suit. Why cavil? – I am beautiful!
We smile – but it has taken all these years to realize
That when I looked at Einstein he saw me.

At last that May when Germany collapsed
The British kidnapped Heisenberg from France
Where he and colleagues sat in a special transit camp
Named "Dustbin," to save them from a threat they never knew:
A mad American general thought to solve
The post-war nuclear problem by having them all shot.

Some boys in pristine uniforms crowd the car
(West Pointers fleeing from a weekend dance?),
Youth's ambiguities resolved in a single action.
I still see their faces in the yellow light
As the train jolts, then starts up again,
So many destined never to be men.

In Cambridge the Germans visited old friends
Kept apart by war: Austrians, English, Danes,
"In a happy reunion at Farm Hall."
But then the giant fist struck – in the still
Center of chaos, noise unimaginable, we thought we heard
The awful cry of God.

Hiroshima. Heisenberg at first refused
To believe it, till the evening news confirmed
That their work had led to Hiroshima's 100,000 dead.
"Worst hit of us all," said Heisenberg, "was Otto Hahn,"
Who discovered uranium fission. "Hahn withdrew to his room,
And we feared that he might do himself some harm."

It is exactly noon, and Doctor Einstein
Is an ancient drawing of the sun.
Simple as a saint emerging from his cell
Dazed by his own light. I think of Giotto, Chaucer,
All good and moral medieval men
In – yet removed from – their historic time.

The week before we heard of Heisenberg
My parents and I are chatting on the train
From Washington. A grey-haired handsome man
Listens with open interest, then inquires
If he might join us. We were such a fascinating family!
"Oh yes," we chorus, "sit with us!"

Penn Station near at hand, we asked his name.
E.O. Lawrence, he replied, and produced his card.
I'd never heard of him, but on an impulse asked,
"What is all this about harnessing
Of the sun's rays? Should we be frightened?"
He smiled. "My dear, there's nothing in it."

So reassured, we said goodbyes,
And spoke of him in coming years, that lovely man.
Of course we found out who he was and what he did,
At least as much as we could comprehend.
Now I am living in the Berkeley hills,
In walking distance of the Lawrence Lab.

Here where Doctor Lawrence built the cyclotron,
It's noon: the anniversary of Hiroshima:
Everywhere, all over Japan
And Germany, people are lighting candles.
It's dark in Germany and Japan, on different days,
But here in Berkeley it is twelve o'clock.

I stand in the center of the library
And he appears. Are we witnesses or actors?
The old man and the girl, smiling at one another,
He fixed by fame, she fluid, still without identity.
An instant which changes nothing.
And everything, forever, everything is changed.

Parents' Pantoum

Where did these enormous children come from,
More ladylike than we have ever been?
Some of ours look older than we feel.
How did they appear in their long dresses

More ladylike than we have ever been?
But they moan about their aging more than we do,
In their fragile heels and long black dresses.
Thet say they admire our youthful spontaneity.

They moan about their aging more than we do,
A somber group – why don't they brighten up?
Though they say they admire our youthful spontaneity
They beg us to be dignified like them

As they ignore our pleas to brighten up.
Someday perhaps we'll capture their attention
Then we won't try to be dignified like them
Nor they to be so gently patronizing.

Someday perhaps we'll capture their attention.
Don't they know that we're supposed to be the stars?
Instead they are so gently patronizing.
It makes us feel like children – second-childish?

Perhaps we're too accustomed to be stars,
The famous flowers glowing in the garden,
So now we pout like children. Second-childish?
Quaint fragments of forgotten history?

Our daughters stroll together in the garden,
Chatting of news we've chosen to ignore,
Pausing to toss us morsels of their history,
Not questions to which only we know answers.

Eyes closed to news we've chosen to ignore,
We'd rather excavate old memories,
Disdaining age, ignoring pain, avoiding mirrors.
Why do they never listen to our stories?

Because they hate to excavate old memories
They don't believe our stories have an end.
They don't ask questions because they dread the answers.
They don't see that we've become their mirrors,

We offspring of our enormous children.

FOR MAXINE KUMIN

Arthur's Party

I came with some trepidation to your vernissage
Knowing your palette: bellicose neon rainbows
Staining the white walls of our old garage.
But who looked at paintings? Elbow nudging elbow,
Your friends and I were exchanging persiflage.

One of Mother's favorite words was "persiflage,"
So I swore one day I'd put it in a poem. Here,
Mom! Many and many's the Village vernissage
We attended, she and I, exchanging badinage –
Another good one! we said, sewing togas in our garage.

I put on plays for the neighborhood in that garage:
Hamlet – its end a stageful of limp doll's bodies;
Then Comedy Tiime: my improv, my leaden persiflage.
(What a tedious child I was!) You painted sets with brio.
But now is now: we return to your vernissage.

Your friends grab wine from trays at the vernissage
Where color strangles color – rude, avenging rainbows!
As badinage grows more vulgar, more blurry the persiflage.
But you'll succeed one day. Be patient. (Ha!) My mother
Fingered you young, as we played in our garage.

In Hell with Virg and Dan

"Yo, Dan, just give a look at this repulsive creature
Called Fraud, the wall-buster; He's the prime polluter.
The poison in his tail's an added feature."
Then Virgil gave the high sign to that stink
Of rottenness, to make a three-point landing on the shore.
But he told it not too near that awesome brink.
It sunk its head and chest but not its tail.

10.   Its face was mellow, friendly-like, and human,
But like a great big ugly snake its torso;
Hair to its armpits like a hippie, only more so.
Its front and back were covered with some weird design
Tatooed with knots and circles to the hip, he
Shone like a rainbow or embroidery, just so fine
No third-world Turk or Tartar stitched it better

18.   Or the Spider Woman spun a thinner line.
Then like a boat half-beached and half in water,
Or when they're home, gross Germans overeat

22.   Or a beaver waits for prey (*but Dan, it was an otter*)
That squalid monster lay where shore and water meet.
Its poisoned tail was quivering in the empty air.
Now my leader told me, "Just direct your feet
To where you're closer to that crouching Geryon."
No way to duck my fate. I had to carry on.
Though, man, I was terrified not paranoid.
We stuck to the right, took ten steps round the bend,
Trying to dodge the sand and fire – but then I saw

36.   Some ways on, a bunch of dudes that sat like in a spell.
Then Virg says, "Go check out those moneylenders
So you'll learn the score about this ring of Hell.
And while you're rapping with them, I'll cajole
Old Geryon, to see if it will lift us
Out of here on its humongous shoulders.

2.

But make it quick. This is no place to stick around."
So all on my own I crept along the strand
Of the Seventh Circle where those sad jerks hung out,
46. Weeping cascades, lifting their butts off the burning ground.
They slapped at the flames or at the red-hot sand
Like dogs in summer, with their paws and snouts
Trying to fend off gnats or fleas or flies.
I stared like hard at all their fire-scorched faces
And I didn't recognize a single man.
55. But I saw a purse that was hung round every neck,
Each one with a fancy color and design,
That all those wretched creeps were grooving on
As if each pouch was good enough to chew.
One yellow purse was stamped with a turquoise lion;
Then I saw on another chest a bag all bloody red
That showed a goose pale as oleo or sweet butter.
A guy with a white purse showing a pregnant sow
65. Turned on me with a ferocious mutter:
"Get the hell out of Hell, and do it now!
Ditch this ditch – but since you're alive I'll tell you
My old pal, Vitaliano, will pretty soon be dead;
He'll sit on my left. Meanwhile these fucking Florentines
– and me a Paduan! – keep screaming in my ear,
72. 'Let's hear it for that awesome cavalier
Who wears a purse with three goats printed on it.'"
He twisted his ugly lips, stuck out his tongue at them
Like an ox that licks his nose. I thought I'd better split
Before my peerless leader chewed me out.
And Virg had climbed aboard. "Don't let your nerve fail.
82. We gotta go down this scary flight of stairs.
Hop on in front, away from that vicious tail."
I'm shaking like a guy who croaks from fever,
His fingernails already turned blue-white,
At the thought of a place where there's no sunlight ever.

3.

From Virgil's words I'm so panicked I'm passing out.
Because he's so gutsy though, I'm struggling to be brave
90. Like a junior camper facing an Eagle Scout.
So I climbed on and clung to those scaley shoulders
And tried to say – but the words wouldn't come out right –
"I'm begging, Virgil baby, hold me tight!"
I knew I could count on Virg when things got scary;
He'd saved my ass a few times before this.
He hugs me close, goes, "Get a move on, Gery!
Sail in wide circles, retract your landing gear
As we sink with this new load you have to carry."
It slipped, inch by inch, off the edge of the abyss
100. Like a big ship sliding from its moorings;
And when it had backed enough to feel in the clear,
Geryon took off, went spinning in a circle
Till its chest was where its tail had been before,
Stretched out that eely tail, using it to steer,
Gathered up the air in its huge paws.
No one had ever been more scared than I was,
Not even Phaeton when he let go the sun-car's reins
And scorched the sky – the scars still seen in the Milky Way;
Not even Icarus, wings falling off as he neared the sun
110. When the wax that held them on had begun to melt,
And his old man yelled, "You've gone too far!" That's how
    I felt.
Nothing but air around me, nothing to be seen
Except for horrible Gery, swimming, swimming down,
And me so petrified I've turned from white to green.
Geryon wheels, starts to descend, but all I know
Is the wind that slams my face, and I hear the horrible roar
Of a giant whirlpool – like an idiot I look down:
Then I get one heavy case of acrophobia,
Sweating as I hang on even tighter than before.
But landing is worse than flying: I see fire and I hear sobs.
124. That whirlpool is boiling blood, like old Khomeini's
    fountain.

4.

Gery spirals for a touchdown. Around us screeching mobs
Of pain and terror: evil coming nearer, nearer, nearer...
Like an exhausted raptor, a falcon that won't quit
Though all day it hasn't spotted anything to capture
Until its trainer cries, "Come down!" – releasing it
To fall from the sky; but the big bird won't go near
Its master: weary, sulking, perched far off on a jagged stone:
That's how horrible Geryon acts as it sets us down.

And, man, when it unloads, it's outta there, like gone.

NUMBERING: I've numbered according to Dante's lines, but if you're a
compulsive counter you'll notice that some of the numbers are missing.
That's because occasionally I've conflated two lines into one. Dante gets
a bit long-winded from time to time, while I am noted for my concision.

LINE 22: Dante messed up here. He should have said an *otter*. So I
threw in an editorial comment in brackets. Dan thought these animals
fished with their tails, which nicely expands his metaphor even though
it isn't true.

LINE 46: *Nobody else* (poets, that is) has translated that phrase about
the usurers raising their rear ends from the burning sands. (See Single-
ton's notes.) Tsk.

LINES 55–66: Who cares about a bunch of corrupt dudes who lived
700 years ago? Oh all right, so they're the Gianfigliazzi, the Obriachi, the
Scrovegni – and the Umbriago (just kidding).

LINE 72: This is (sigh) Giovanni Buiamonte dei Becchi. Dante is going
in for some heavy irony here: the Florentines heaping honors on this
piece of scum.

LINE 124: I couldn't resist referring to the late Ayatollah's attractive
Fountain of Blood in Teheran's cemetery. An old failing of mine. Sorry
about that.

Lost in Translation

"Why wouldn't she entertain her nephew?
There has to be a reason in the story."
Mr. Chuck, who translates, wouldn't translate
Or couldn't. He says the brilliant Chinese novelist
Seems to say the nephew doesn't matter.

"There has to be a reason for the nephew."
I don't think that Mr. Chuck is trying.
"She denies there is a lesbian component
In this story of a friendship between women."
I grow impatient. "That's really not the issue.

"A friendship between two such different women,
One older, lonely, the other, kind, gregarious – "
I challenge Mr. Chuck to translate *that* –
"Seems to founder on the issue of the nephew."
He says she says the nephew's not important.

"But when the nephew asks if he may visit,
And the older woman doesn't want to bother,
Though the other urges her to be adventurous,
Reach out! befriend the young! – that's not important?"
"There is nothing homosexual in the story."

"I didn't say there was!" I'm getting cranky.
As the novelist talks more, he translates less.
(What kind of crazy Chinese name is Chuck?)
"Isn't the cooling of the women's friendship
Due to their differing views about the nephew?"

The friendship ends because the older woman
Learns that her friend has had a married lover
When she had thought they were celibate together.
"There is nothing homosexual about it."
"But, Goddammit, what about the nephew?

"A writer doesn't just throw in a nephew
For no good reason. He must advance the story.
Are you saying that Lacan *et cie* are right,
That the author doesn't know what she is doing
Until the critic condescends to tell us?"

The brilliant Chinese novelist is famous
Especially for "One on One," this story.
Mr. Chuck is just an old-time Chinese journalist
Who smiles opaquely at the two articulate women
Snagged on the barbed wire of the language barrier.

He doesn't care. It's only a couple of women
Trying to discuss another pair of women.
His part is to neuter this conversation.
No sex! Especially no homosexuality.
He, not the nephew, is just an old Red herring.

FOR LU XING'ER

Cultural Evolution

after Pope

When from his cave, young Mao in his youthful mind
A work to renew old China first designed,
Then he alone interpreted the law,
And from traditional fountains scorned to draw:
But when to examine every part he came,
Marx and Confucius turned out much the same.

Four Translations:

A Present for Tu Fu from Li Po

Last time we met
on the mountain top
in the noonday sun,
you in the shade of
your preposterous hat

you were much plumper
than you are now.
Perhaps you were
pregnant with poems?

Maryam

by Ingeborg Bachman

From whom did you inherit your dark hair
And the almond sound of your sweet name?
It isn't youth that makes you gleam of dawn.
From an Eastern land for a thousand years you came.

Promise us Jericho; waken above the Psaltar,
The source of the River Jordan in your hand.
Startle the murderers when you stone them,
And, in a moment, see your second land!

Every stony breast you touch, a miracle;
Every teardrop slipping down the stone.
Be self-baptized with the steaming water.
Stay alien till we are alien to our own.

Often, snow will fall into your cradle,
Beneath its rockers the groan of ice in thaw.
Sleep deep enough, the world will be your captive.
The waters of the Red Sea will withdraw!

What is True

by Ingeborg Bachman

Truth kicks no sand into your eyes,
Truth required of you by death and sleep
As if carved in flesh, prompted by agonies,
Truth rolls back the boulder from your tomb.

Truth – so subterranean and faded
In leaf and kernel, in your tongue's lazy bed
A year, another year, year after year –
Truth does not make Time, it leaves it dead.

Truth parts the earth, combs out the dreaming,
Combs out the braided wreath and all the leavings,
It twirls its comb, knocks into you
The ripened crops, drains you completely.

Truth's never quelled till it is looted,
Which is perhaps for you the crucial way.
Where wounds appear, you are its booty;
It overtakes you only to betray.

Here comes the moon with sour tankards.
Drink up! In the fall of bitter night
Not a single twig is rescued,
Foam flakes the dove into a feathered flight.

Loaded with chains, the world is your encumbrance
But truth is driving cracks into the wall.
As you grow you search the dark for what is righteous,
Facing the obscure exit of your cell.

Tirade for the Next-to-Last Act

by Nina Cassian

I'm leaving you, I won't touch you anymore.
I've run out of things I have to prove to you,
so there's no reason to postpone the drowning
of molecules called hands or eyes or mouth
in the patient earth which waits – but not for me.
Earth knows it owns me, right to horizon-zero.
I've told you almost everything I know;
even the lie I told was a pious lie
because it leapt to life, came into being
embodied as a leaf, or as a rabbit,
and I cannot reject a living creature.
Also, I leave you because I am so weary
of the way the century melts in the one before
as if the milk the child sucks from its mother
went back into her breast – or worse than that,
as if the brow of a philosopher
kept sloping back till it rejoined a species
long extinct, and hirsute, and prehensile.

I've picked up information on my way
but none of it from scholarly pursuits
or from the established canon of great books;
mostly from heat and cold, from birth and death,
all that comes past us only once, alas,
so it's no guide for what will happen next.
I remain as vulnerable as ever,
knowing a thousand objects by their names,
a thousand states of mind I cannot name.
I don't see their utter metamorphoses,
I didn't notice when they took their leave,
abandoning me to confusion,
as if dropped into a pool of blood.
So I'm leaving; I won't touch you anymore.
You've said so many times you can't abide me
though I drew my portrait for you with such care,

relying on the way you had sketched it out.
But I'm incapable of imitation,
or so it seems. I lack the talent
to resemble you – much less, myself.

My smiles are always misconstrued as grins,
And when I laugh, all heads are turned away
as if I had committed some indecency.
I pick the wrong occasions for my tears:
when the crowd cheers a city holiday.
When I sculpt a statue, everyone screams,
"He has made himself into a graven image!"
When I shrivel with a serious illness,
I'm not believed: it's the devious way
my sad body causes an obscure epidemic…
So I'm leaving you, goodbye. I'm gone. Goodbye.

Medicine

When the nurses, interns, doctors came running full tilt down the hall,
Dragging the crash-cart with shrieking wheels and flagless IV pole,
And that squat box, the defibrillator, made to jolt the heart;

Then we next-of-kin, pasted against the walls, ran after them
To your room, Mother-in-Law, where they hammered hard
    on your chest,
Forcing you back to life in which you had no further interest.

For the third time they pressed like lovers on your frail bones
To restart the beat. They cheered! Marked you alive on your chart,
Then left you, cold, incontinent, forlorn.

When the man loved by you and me appealed to your doctor
To know why you couldn't have your way and be let go,
He said, "I couldn't just stand there and watch her die."

Later, when it was over, we spoke to a physician
Grown grey and wise with experience, our warm friend,
But ice when he considers the rigors of his profession,

And repeated to him your young death-doctor's reply,
We heard the stern verdict no lesser person could question:
But that was his job: to just stand there and watch her die.

FOR JOHN MURRAY

48

Poem for Your Birthday

This year both our birthdays end in zero,
Symbol, perhaps, of the nothing we'll become
Except as the reflections of our children –
Your boys, my girls, – in the next millenium
Now so near. Who thought we'd see it come?

Let us reflect awhile on us, my dear:
Born fortunate, two creatures petted and well-fed
With milk and vitamins, thus our good teeth and skin;
Curled hair and handmade clothes and patent slippers,
This side of the moat from the desperate unemployed.

Ah yes! – and hasn't that come round again!
We circle back to the fascinating question:
How did we get from there to where we are?
We've perched on the edge of revolution, war,
I, in China, you, in Pakistan.

We both knew children who have died by fire.
We're yoked in sympathy for all that's human,
Having loved those of every tone of skin,
Having lived the loss of extraordinary men.

And the poems we've read aloud to one another!
You wave you arms in a wide arc of rapture,
Moved by the Muse and another glass of wine.
I cherish that characteristic gesture
As you must smile at some oddity of mine.

Truly to relish trivia in flower,
Woman-talk of recipes and clothes,
One must be aware of that high discourse
On art and life we could deal with if we chose.

"The flow of soul," as Pope extravagantly called it,
Unstopped, though years of parting intervene,
Though illness, duties, children interrupt,
We know we'll go on talking till the end

Or after, when we still reach out in thought,
Or waking, sense the living person near.
The password at the boundary is *Friend*.

FOR BARBARA THOMPSON

Marriage Song

with commentary

We begin with the osprey who cries, "Clang, clang!"
Which is the sound of the door of marriage slamming.
Our metaphor sits on a nest, surrounded
By blooming succulents; ospreys like swans, mate once.
For form's sake they appear in public together;
Because she and her spouse play separate roles
They will forego connubial bliss if necessary
To save their feathered souls.

Complementary image: young, pale, scared,
Has menstruated once, sequestered in a cave,
Miss Chou Dynasty, under lock and key
Thus to preserve her sacred chastity,
Knows that someday her Prince will come.
But this occurs between stanzas two and three.
Thus far she is only a dream in his questing eye.
He doesn't come, he just breathes heavily.

The principal commentaries differ here:
Mao-fang believes the lady tossed from side to side
In bed with long long thoughts of separation.
A respected version claims that the aging bride
Dutifully tried to recruit the limberest dames
For her still-randy spouse, states earnestly
That she worried about the good ones getting away
– or so the followers of Confucius say.

But what, Students, was the intention of the Poem
Before the moral scholiasts worked it over?
The text obscure: was it maid or matron here?
Did not our Princess roll from side to side
Alone with long long thoughts of her absent lover,
Reluctant, yes, to pick out next year's successor
Yet feeling perhaps it was better to marry *and* burn
Than to stay yearning in that cave forever.

Now cry desire, shake silver tambourines
To cue the strings of gypsy violins
As the Fisher-Prince mates with his fluttering Bride.
O her chaste joy! She will hold him in her bosom
(suckle her spouse in dream), then toss and turn…
The girls glide out of reach like water-lilies
Slipping along the current of the stream.
Though Pound and Waley speak of zither and gong
In truth our modest heroine bursts into song:

"Alone, I become virginal again.
I know the cave, I learn the cave within.
And you, my Lord, are somewhere out of reach.
I hear your breathy sigh: the aging man
Tuning his lute in our remotest room.
Beside myself at last, I think and think
Of ospreys on their island, dark of wing,
Snow-breasted, and transfixed in abstract love."

Index, a Mountain

(Part of the Cascade range, Washington state.)

Early one day a mountain uprose, all cased in silver
Where morning fog caught in the tips of cedars
And a moon-colored sun polished virgin timber.

As Red Freddie, our old new Studebaker
Steams over the Cascades, Mother says to Father,
"I wanted to bring you here on our honeymoon;
First growth. Never cut over." In my fifth year,
Carsick on hairpin turns, bribed not to chatter
A penny a mile; the black-timbered Inn at the summit
Where I roll out and under the bed at night,
Awake, screaming with claustrophobia,
Clawing the bedsprings, having dreamed
Me in my coffin.

Motoring on at dawn, to Index then we came:
A cut muscle. A smoking cinder.

An old bald lumberman had cut God's finger,
Himself missing a limb. (As usual, Retribution
didn't know when to quit, took the whole arm.)
One day he'll appear, on 16 millimeter film,
Bracing his brassie between one stump
And a tough left arm.
The drive sails down the fairway, hooking slightly.
He gloats; a ghostly hand pinned to his shoulder.
Twenty years have passed, and I, all unknowing,
Have married the grandson of this predator.

O friends and our descendants, what remains?
Banquets of sawdust, hazy leisure bought
From the swink of loggers and the stink of pulp;
Victorian mansions ugly as the mills
Bulldozed for malls, car stalls defined
By rows and rows of scruffy little trees.

Preserve nothing! The simple motto of our frontier
Because men choked on green, were suffocated
By a press of trees, fire was their liberator.
Fire went too far, like Retribution,
Like any Revolution. Revenge has a long finger.

O Pioneers, who stripped the earth so fast,
Who toiled so hard Imagination failed.
How could you dream of the later Marxist
Trailblazers, enshrining worker-heroes
On their plinths of crumbling concrete,
Giant fingers that pierced the ancient ceiling
Scarred with the junk of her astronauts and ours?
Our icons: Lenin, Bunyan: Peter and Paul
Like Barnum pointing, "This way to the Egress,"
To be saved from our follies by fleeing to the stars.

2.

Ours is a world full of finger-worship
As the holy Roman bone-collectors knew:
Keepers of femur and tibia, toenail sniffers
Their artisans formed silver reliquaries,
Cool tubes, like those that encase a good cigar,
To hold erect the dust of an index finger.

Now, for history, we drive a car
From the empty summit (the old inn long burned down)
Past Troublesome Creek to Goldbar, a mining camp
Where a few Chinese were saved from an early riot
By shipping them out-of-town in slapped-up coffins,
To Sultan, where they lit the lamps at three
In the afternoon, woods were so dense.
Lilacs were as large as fruit trees once;
Houses of pioneers, with weathered siding,
Looked like birds' nests fallen among the cedars,
Such great dark brooding trees they were!

The barren shade of the high Cascades ends here.
It's all burned-over, pocked with stumps that look
Like the old man's arm. The view, as we descend,
blending to smooth pasture, pastoral landscape
dotted with cows, gives way to golf-course lawns,
a strident green, bobbed willows, men on carts.
While just outside the gates a sign proclaims,
"The Wages of Sin is Death!" A finger aimed at *you*.

This West! full of crank religions, bleeding atoners,
Raw, shapeless women, stringy men with tracts
on your porch at dawn, wanting to play you a record.
The pulp they press on us with bony fingers
Conceiving us in Sin, had its own conception
In the sawmill's sweet dust – pressed from our trees!

O Index, naked mountain, with your scarred flanks
Still your raw summit points to heaven.
Serve as God's tombstone. Have no green mercy on us.

A Song for Muriel

No one explains me because
There is nothing to explain.
It's all right here
Very clear.
O for my reputations sake
To be difficult, and opaque!

No one explains me because
Though myopic, I see plain.
I just put it down
With a leer and a frown ...
Why does it make you sweat?
Is this the thanks I get?

No one explains me because
There are tears in my bawdy song.
Once I am dead
Something will be said.
How nice I won't be here
To see how they get it wrong.

Anniversaries:
Claremont Avenue, from 1945

I'm sitting on a bench at One Hundred and Fifteenth
and Riverside Drive, with my books beside me,
early for my lesson in Chinese
at Twenty-One Claremont, right around the corner.
Two little girls pass in front of me
wheeling a doll carriage, fussing
with the doll and the doll blanket: then casually
one of them says,"the President is dead,"
pulling the coverlet over the doll's head.
The other replies in a flat little voice, "Yes,
the President is dead." I think, "Strange children
who toy with the notion of mortality!"

Wind sweeps from the Hudson. Chill. It's time to go.
In the lobby I press the button for the elevator;
at last it clanks to a stop, the doors slide open
and I confront the seamed black face of Joe
runneled with tears. So I know it's true:
The President is dead. We rise in silence
past the floor where a lonely boy may play
those holidays when he's freed from boarding school.
Thirty years later almost to the day
I'll marry him, in a church eight blocks away.

The elevator groans to the fifth floor.
Bliss, the gentle Chinese wife, opens the door,
her smile faint in the lotus of her face.
My teacher, Chen, expressionless. We start the lesson
as if nothing unusual had occurred,
then fall silent. Bliss brings the balm of tea,
exquisite Bliss who, ten years further on
will hang herself in their pale-blue bedroom
with one of Chen's ties.
Before our tea is cool my Mother comes
smiling and weeping. Though the President and she

are of an age, like Bliss and me
she has lost the father
who'd almost seen us through a war.

When Mother and I take the Seventh Avenue subway
the cars are stuffed with people black and white;
strangers murmur to strangers, strangers crying
as they clutch their papers, headlines black on white.
There's comfort here, but it's cold as we straggle out
in the dark, to Sheridan Square.
Later my first sister-in-law will tell me
that at Vassar, girls were dancing on the tables
cheering the news – an alien breed of stranger.
I'm glad I wasn't there
but with the bereaved on Seventh Avenue.

In the eighties we go to stay with my husband's Mother,
this cultivated student of art history
and liturgical music. She is a baseball nut
comparing notes with Joe as they watch TV.
Chen, who is friends with no one, reappears
in the Claremont lobby, after thirty years
and invites us for a drink.
As the elevator labors up I am suffused
with memories of Bliss: Bliss and her taste:
celadon walls, peach-blossom silk embroidery,
jade objects on the tables, jade
on her wrists, a flower at her throat,
that porcelain throat....
Bliss and your incense, your pleading tremulous heart.

At six, Chen answers the bell
and we step into a cavern grim as hell:
bare boards, a cot with dirty sheets,
card table, metal folding chair – and that is all.
In great grey swags, wallpaper peels from the walls,
a stack of *Wall Street Journals* in the corner.
Where are the carpets, the bibelots, the scrolls?
All gone, sold or destroyed. A bottle of whiskey

and three tumblers sit on the rickety table.
Miserable, we stand awkwardly and drink
while Chen tells us he's gambled it all away;
matter-of-factly says what we don't care to hear:
how in their final years Bliss and he
could only masturbate each other.
I bless my husband's upright stone-faced Mother.

It's 1985: in pain, my Mother-in-law has died.
Appraisers from Doyle pick through her possessions:
old furniture blistered by sun and central heat.
Twenty-One Claremont is no longer ours.
Recollections are blistered and faded too:
My husband's boyhood toys, my fragments of Chinese.
Mothers have disappeared. Wars come and go.
The past is present: what we choose to keep
by a process none of us can ever know.
Now those little girls are grandmothers
who must remember, after fifty years
the doll, the chill, the tears.
Greatness felled at a blow.
Memory fractured. Black and white apart.
No sense of direction, we Americans.
No place to go.

Fin-de-Siècle Blues

I.

At seventeen I'm told to write a paper
on "My Philosophy": unconscious Emersonian
clone, courtesy of my Father,
"There is no evil," that's what I say,
"merely the absence of good." I read the papers.
Where was my head? (In the clouds, like Father
and the senior William James.) I must have known
some of the bad news. No evil, eh?
Ho, Ho, Ho, Holocaust! Tell it to the Jews.

I wrote another paper, worrying
about the fate of historic monuments,
Art, not people, during World War II.
Give me that tired query from Ethics 101
concerning the old lady and a Rembrandt etching
in a sinking rowboat: which one would I save?
Now that I *am* one, still I have serious doubts
about saving the old lady.
Rembrandt would have won.
And if they could have been crammed into the rowboat
so would the French cathedrals and the Parthenon.
(There was some kind of screaming aesthete
Naked within my transparent ethical overcoat.)

But now, take Sarajevo: Old ladies, buildings,
children, art; all perish together
along with honor and philosophy;
the hypothetical rowboat long since sunk
in the polluted Mediterranean sea.
The century suffers entropy – and so do I.

II.

Well, it's been one hell of a century:
Endless lists of victims, Armenians, Jews,
Gypsies, Russians, Vietnamese,
the Bosnians, the Somalians,
torture and rape of the dissidents all over
the map; and as Time winds down
the music slows,
grows scratchier, plays off-key,
America chimes in with its own obbligatos:
what we did to the Nicaraguans, the Salvadorians,
diminuendos with Granadans, Panamanians –
and we're still hassling poor old Castro.

Whole continents go on living under tyrannies
till tyrannies give way
to chaos and criminality.
Is it the horror, or that we know
about the horror – this evening's blood
on the screen?
Yugoslavia, before our eyes, is Balkanized
to death; but today, brave us,
today we recognized Macedonia.
(Vasco is dead, thank God,
and how are you faring, dear Bogomil?)

Then we have AIDS...
Maurice, Tom, Tony, Gordon, Jim, Peter, Bill,
bitterly I mourn you
and wait for the next beloved name.
The red-neck senators who would starve the Arts
are a less efficient scourge.
We who are merely witnesses
to all this grief
also pay a price.
NOT AN ORIGINAL THOUGHT
(that's part of the price).

Horror numbs.
Violence, whether fictional or true,
is socially addictive.
NOT AN ORIGINAL THOUGHT
Serious satire undermined
by sexual and political
grotesquerie.
NOT AN ORIGINAL THOUGHT
So why go on? I'm blue. Boo-hoo.
Got those End-of-the-Century blues.

III.

Now to personalize and trivialize the topic,
As writers, what are we to do?
We gag on scandal, our lives are gossip fodder.
In our marginal way, we are becoming stars.
Never mind the work. Who cares for that?
Did the man who reinvented the sonnet
urinate in his bed one night when drunk?
Did our great fat nature poet
throw up in his hat?
Forget the revolution they created
with their raw confessional poetry;
it's the suicides of two women
which fascinate,
not their way of working
but their way of death.

O you serious men and women
who wrote your poems, met your classes,
counseled your students, kept your friends
and sent magic letters home,
your lives are pillaged and rearranged
by avid biographers who boast that they tell all,
so it seems you always reeled in a mad whirl
of alcohol, abandonment and sexual betrayal.
(I sorrow for the stain on your memory,

Anne, Randall, Ted, Elizabeth,
Delmore, John, and Cal.)

As writers, what are we to do?
Our roles as witnesses ignored,
our fine antennae blunted
by horror piled on horror,
our private matters open
to the scrutiny of voyeurs.
If we have wit and learning
it's met with the apathy
of the ever-more-ignorant young.
How do we hope to carry on
in the last gasp of the millenium?

Much as we always have: writing for one another,
for the friends we tried to impress in school
(like Tonio Krüger), for the dead father or mother,
for our first mentor, compassionate and cool,
for the dead authors who watch over us.
We'll write when bored in strange hotel rooms,
we'll write when the conscience pricks,
we'll write from passion, present or reviving,
making copy of our pains or perverse kicks.
We'll write if a cookie dipped in tea
transports us to the fields of memory.

But first of all we'll do it for ourselves,
selfish and narcissistic and obsessed as ever,
invading the privacy of those who care for us,
spilling sad secrets confided by a lover.
We take note of the café where Valéry took notes,
Van Gogh's yellow chair, the monastery
where Murasaki wrote, as Petrarch did,
in a room eight feet by three;
Name-and place-dropping, grooming our fur,
Fanning and shaking our peacock tails
(dry sticks rattling in the wind),
always, always ourselves our own mirrors.

The burden of our song: good luck to the young!
Let's drink (for we drink) to a better world
for them, if they should live so long.
As my father the optimist used to say,
"It's the unexpected that happens."
There is little point in being fatalistic;
Whatever occurs will be different from
what we anticipate,
which, to be frank, is universal doom.

Everyone who reads this is older than Mozart,
than Masaccio, than Keats, much older than Chatterton.
We're taller, handsomer, healthier than they.
So let's just count these years we've lived as velvet
as Carver said at the end – sweet Ray.
I'm blessed by parents, children, husband, friends
for now... Nothing can take that away.
NOT AN ORIGINAL THOUGHT
Call up Voltaire. Tend the garden.
Seize the day.

Notes

GERDA:

The epigraph to this poem is from an old Swedish children's prayer, circa 1780, from which I've omitted the final couplet: "Lycken kommer, lycken gar. / Du förbliver Fader var," which can be translated as:

> God, who loves little children,
> Take care of this small person.
> Wherever I wander in the world
> My fate lies in your hands.
> Fortune comes and goes
> But You are our Father forever.

So much more comforting, I would say, than "If I should die before I wake…"

AN AMERICAN BEAUTY:

The ERA, for those who are very young or who have short memories, stands for the Equal Rights Amendment, for which Ms London did the research and wrote the legislation.

TWELVE O'CLOCK

The inspiration for this poem came from an article in *The San Francisco Chronicle* about the widow of the late physicist, E.O. Lawrence, including a photograph of a very beautiful old lady. Mary Lawrence was trying to have her husband's name removed from the Lawrence-Livermore Lab, where some of the most horrendous experiments with "nuclear devices" are carried out. She felt this was a desecration of her husband's name and philosophy. I involved myself in this effort, to no avail. But Mrs. Lawrence had become a muse of mine. I, who had never taken anything other than a general science course in high school, began to study books on physics. I kept up this reading for about two years – not scientific tomes but popular accounts.

When I began to write the poem there were a number of things I wanted to accomplish. First, the dialectic of the poem: the belief of my mother and Einstein in an essentially orderly universe, versus Heisenberg's and my belief in a universe that is random and disorderly. Second, I wanted the poem to reflect Einstein's concept of simultaneity: everything happens at once! Third, I wanted the poem to be a piece of autobiography: to include everything – pathetically little – that I had ever thought or heard about atomic physics and physicists. Therefore nothing is invented; every quote is from memory. Though my memory is faulty in many respects, I have a clear recollection of what has been said to me.

In Hell with Virg and Dan:

Canto XVII was originally commissioned by the Ecco Press for its excellent volume of translations of Dante by contemporary poets. My contribution was quite properly rejected for irreverence and "not fitting in." I just don't care for Dante's obsessions with shit and revenge. For me, he ranks up there with St. Paul as one of the most destructive literary geniuses of all time. Dante had a lot better sense of humor though.

Tirade for the Next to Last Act:

A few teachers have been interested in one of my techniques for translation, both to avoid writing "translatese" and to loosen up: It consists of writing in what I've named "Antique Hipster." As you can see by my version of Dante, I stayed in that mode! But with the Cassian piece, I was able to convert to a straight poem. However, by popular request of at least three people, I include the hipster version which I trust Nina Cassian – that noble poet – will never see:

> I'm splitting, so long, no way I'll get in touch.
> Like, man, I've got nothing more to prove,
> So why hang around for the drowning
> of those molecules called, like, hands or eyes or mouth
> in the dirt that doesn't hang around or want me.
> That dirt knows its got me, out to the zero rim.
> I've spilled my guts, blabbed everything I know
> and when I lie it's 'cause I'm queer for piety:
> I see that dumb lie come to life and get a body

Like some dumb leaf, or some dumb bunny –
and I dig anything alive.
Also I'm splitting 'cause I'm fuckin' sick
of seeing this century sink into the one before
as if the milk the kid sucks from its mom's tit
flows right back into mom – or worse yet,
like, if the forehead of some heavy thinker
kept sloping back till it got to be, like, extinct,
some kinda throwback, all hairy, like, prehensile.

I figured out some stuff along the way:
not like that shit they shovel you in school,
a long way from that holy Great Books junk,
but the dope that you pick up from cold and heat,
birth, death, and all that jazz –
everything you get a shot at only once
so it's no use for whatever comes down next.
So here I am without any skin,
knowing the names for, like, a thousand things,
without a clue as to what they're really called.
And I don't know when they take off or how they change,
and I'm, like, floundering around
as if I swam in some damn pool of blood.
So I'm splitting; I won't ever get in touch.
You've said a bunch of times that you can't stand me
though I drew you a picture of me, super-careful,
just like you would have drawn it by yourself.
But, man, I'm no good at imitations,
I got no skill, no talent
to try to look like you, or even me.

Now when I give with a smile, nobody gets it:
They think it's, like, a leer.
And when I giggle, people turn their backs
as if I'd crawled out of a porno-flick.
And I always bawl at the wrong times: like
it's some bogus patriotic holiday. I make a statue
and they scream some crap about graven images.
When I'm, like, shriveling up – like, terminal,

it's supposed to be some kind of a sick joke,
like my sad body's trying to start an epidemic.
So, man, I'm gone; I'm going, going, gone.

MARRIAGE SONG:

My friend, the distinguished Chinese scholar Jerome Seaton, pointed out to
me two translations of a Chou Dynasty poem, one by Arthur Waley and
one by Ezra Pound. The original song is anonymous, which suggests that it
might well have been composed by a woman. The oddity of these transla-
tions is that one wouldn't know that they referred to the same poem –
other than a reference to "tossing and turning" – and that the Pound ver-
sion is three stanzas long while Waley's is five stanzas. Neither translation
is an example of the best work of these great men, to put it politely. I was
raised on the poems of both of them, and when they are criticized I hasten
to remind all of us of the debt we owe them in their introduction of Asian
poetry to Western readers and writers. Here is Waley's version:

"Fair, fair," cry the ospreys
On the island in the river.
Lovely is this noble lady,
Fit bride for our lord.

In patches grows the water mallow;
To left and right one must seek it.
Shy was this noble lady;
Day and night he sought her,

Sought her and could not get her;
Day and night he grieved.
Long thoughts, oh, long unhappy thoughts,
Now on his back, now tossing on to his side.

In patches grows the water mallow;
To left and right one must gather it.
Shy is this noble lady;
With great zithern and little we hearten her.

68

In patches grows the water mallow;
To left and right one must choose it.
Shy is this noble lady;
With gongs and drums we will gladden her.

And now Pound:

"Hid! Hid!" the fish-hawk saith.
by isle in Ho the fish-hawk saith:
        "Dark and clear,
        Dark and clear,
So shall be the prince's fere."

Clear as the stream her modesty;
As neath dark boughs her secrecy,
        reed against reed
        tall on slight
as the stream moves left and right,
        dark and clear,
        dark and clear.
To seek and not to find
as a dream in his mind,
        think how her robe should be,
        distantly, to toss and turn,
        to toss and turn.

High reed caught in ts'ai grass
        so deep her secrecy;
lute sound in lute sound is caught,
        touching, passing, left and right.
Bang the gong of her delight.

I thought it would be amusing to invent a genre: a poem which would incorporate pseudo-scholarly commentary on the work, from Confucius on down.

Most people will know most of the references, but here is a cast of charac-
ters: PART II: "Vasco" is the great Serbian poet, Vasco Popa (1922–1991),
who was widely believed to be in line for the Nobel Prize when he died,
which we thought untimely, but which saved him from the knowledge of
the death of Yugoslavia. "Bogomil" is the poet and playwright, Bogomil
Gjuzel (1939–) of Macedonia, living in Skopje, whose friends have not
heard from him recently.

"Then we have AIDS": Although I name real people, I prefer to have
them stand for the friends and lovers everyone has lost.

PART III: "The man who reinvented the sonnet": John Berryman; "our
great fat nature poet": Theodore Roethke; "two women" are, of course
Sylvia Plath and Anne Sexton. "Anne, Randall, Ted, Elizabeth, Delmore,
John, and Cal": Anne Sexton again, Randall Jarrell; "Ted": Roethke again;
"Elizabeth": Miss Bishop; "Delmore": Delmore Schwartz; "John": Berry-
man again; "Cal": Robert Lowell.

C. K.

BOOK DESIGN & composition by John D. Berry. The type is Linotype's Post-Script version of Aldus, designed by Hermann Zapf as a book face to accompany Palatino (which was originally intended primarily for display). Aldus was originally issued in metal by Linotype in 1954. *Printed by McNaughton & Gunn.*